Burning Sage

Caitlin Press Inc.
3375 Ponderosa Way
Qualicum Beach, BC V9K 2J8
www.caitlinpress.com

Text design by Vici Johnstone
Cover design by Benjamin Salesse
Printed in Canada

Caitlin Press Inc. acknowledges financial support from the Government of Canada and the Canada Council for the Arts, and the Province of British Columbia through the British Columbia Arts Council and the Book Publisher's Tax Credit.

Library and Archives Canada Cataloguing in Publication

Burning sage : poems from the Lytton fire / Meghan Fandrich.
Fandrich, Meghan, author.
Canadiana 2023020404X | ISBN 9781773861289 (softcover)
LCC PS8611.A5475 B87 2023 | DDC C811/.6,-dc23

Burning Sage

Poems from the Lytton fire

Meghan Fandrich

Caitlin Press 2023

This is my memory of how it happened.
Others will remember it differently; we each have our own truth.
We each have our own story to tell.

For our community,
for Helen,
and for B.

Contents

Take a deep breath in, letting the sweet morning air fill your lungs. Someone is smiling as they sweep the grocery store sidewalk; hear the quick rasp of their broom against the river silt. Look at the thriving garden across the street with its brilliant orange poppies. Notice how their delicate petals tremble in the breeze. A tailgate slams shut. Glance into the farmer's basket as it is carried past you: those fresh-picked greens are so vibrant they could have been painted. Follow them around the corner, just beyond the rainbow crosswalk, where people are laughing and setting up market tables in the cool shade. At one table, a batch of bannock is sizzling as it fries. Try a piece, piping hot, with a layer of homemade huckleberry jam. Savour this Nlaka'pamux comfort food.

Listen to the tinkling wind chimes when a door opens and the inviting smell of espresso pools out. Here, tucked beside the cheerful café, a courtyard garden is alive with lush ivy, fragrant lavender, a flourishing maple. Order your favourite coffee and sit with it for a while as the sun lifts into the sky, its rays warming your skin. Nod at the friendly locals as they pass. Fall into the rhythm of the silvery birdsong. Slow to the pace of this town.

Remember this moment. Breathe in deeply. Feel the beauty of this little place—because tomorrow, it will all be gone.

Entrails

You didn't ask me about it

you weren't like the others
who asked

> aggressive
> bloodthirsty
> cameras rolling

> extracting
> > trauma
> for the consumption of the viewing public

you didn't ask me
about the ash filling the courtyard
the black smudged sky falling heavily into the windows
the man rushing breathlessly through the doorway
> "That fire's really close you gotta go"

you didn't ask me

you don't know about
you didn't
> > see

a tired neighbour peering down the street
looking for the fire
while the hillside behind him
burned

a small child
tripping over summer sandals
pulled by her mother's hand
faster than the wind
faster than the fire

you don't know

that insidious silver shimmer

the sidewalk empty
windows dark

(maybe everyone else is gone)

(maybe they're still home
          shut in
                    oblivious

as the town burns around them)

You didn't ask

4:54 p.m.

I leave the café
and step onto the street

everything is sepia
everything is still

everything is
                    burning

up to the highway
through a thick wall of
yellow-black smoke

driving blind

then
break through

my house below me
        green little oasis

    surrounded by flames

I run things to the car

        a basket of clothes,
        her favourite stuffies,
        the wide-eyed cat

                    a small shift in wind
                    and the house is
                    gone

and back in the car

in the rear-view mirror

a fireball
explodes
across the highway
above my house

Fire at night

I stood on the highway
behind the barricade
and watched the glowing sky
that night

both sides of both rivers
both sides of the mountain between
everything glowing in flame
and the mass of smoke above
glowing red too

somewhere in the dark
was our town
an unknown
probably gone

and somewhere among those flames
were homes, farms
the school
probably burning

that red glow

our whole world
on fire

others watched beside me
their expressionless faces
lit up by the glow

flames reflected in their eyes

we stood together
in silence

and then looked away

At Siska

When everything is burning
there is no cell service
no internet
no connection to the worried world

I am not ok

so I go south
on an empty highway
to find a pocket of reception

messages flood in
by the hundreds

from friends
family
reporters

no

no,
I am not ok

I can't reply
can't focus
so I don't

except to write "we're safe"

my town is gone
my café is gone
my house is likely also gone

I don't know what to do

I am not ok

at the roadside
other locals
check messages too

we hug
say "love you"
but we are not ok

we are not ok

the messages become
too much

so I go north
toward the fire
on an empty highway

I am not ok

Lightning

On the second night
a storm
moves through

every strike
        (there)

means the possibility
of another fire
           (there)

I rush from window to window
looking for flames

(there)

Registration

I cried
the whole way to the city
hours from home
days after the fire

I had to buy toothpaste
got lost in the aisles
shapes blurred into colour
I couldn't

at the evacuation centre
a kind volunteer
tried to fill in my papers

name? yes
birthdate?

I couldn't

so she found it on my licence
told me the date

I nodded
            crumpled

Evacuation

An endless month under smoky skies
sleepless
numb

Helen plays with friends
cared for and loved

and I stumble barefoot through nights and days

Kept away

There is this desperation
to go home
knowing it was saved

empty without us
but full
        with our lives

desperation to go home
knowing it was saved
but not safe

not knowing
when the order will lift
not knowing
what is left

there is this desperate yearning
to go back

    to normal

   to comfort

to life before this happened

Klowa Café

It was a bus tour
for locals, they said
with the rapturous
vulturous
media
following close behind

I didn't go

"I don't need to see it
to know that it's gone"

but a friend
on that bus
sent me a photo

My café

my vibrant little space
with art-filled blue walls
laughter and warmth
community

my courtyard garden
with blooming pink hollyhocks
sunlight, growth, life

my Klowa

my dark basement hole
with crumbling black power poles
broken brick walls
        strewn heavily across the courtyard

my melted glass greenhouse
charred skeleton trees

my blanket of ash

my ruins

I saw the photo
and for the first time
I knew it was gone

Home

We went home
when the order was lifted

drove through fire after fire
a world burning
with fear

found
everything
exactly as I'd left it
a month before

everything
the same
         but dead

no neighbours
no electricity
no water

the smell of old fire
seeping through the windows
at night

I struggled
to make things seem normal
to make home feel safe
when it wasn't

wishing it had burnt too
so I wouldn't have to be there
alone with a child

too devastated
inside the house
to begin to grieve
what was lost
just beyond it

Struggle

We've been home for two weeks
and now ChilkoCat is missing

coyote dreams
coyote in a burned town

Coyote

the whole world is hostile

Awake

The police came to our door
after dark

no streetlights
no neighbours
in this burned-up town

I was expecting them
but jumped
at their midnight
attack

at their flashlights
aimed at my daughter
who clung tightly to my neck

"We're not leaving"
I whispered

fully aware
of the new evacuation order
fully aware of the nearing fire

but this time
I could see it approach
could watch for its glow
could wait for it to crest the hill
above the house
and get too close

with this fire
there was time
for fear

but the fear of leaving again
with nowhere to go
was stronger

. The police stepped back into the night

I stood at the door
in the darkness
and watched for the fire

           fully awake

Main Street

They opened the road
without warning

down the hill
around the corner
the route I'd been dreading since the fire

and there it was

an expanse of wreckage
dotted with chimneys
gutted buildings
broken trees

too surreal
                    to believe

I tried to catch a
glimpse
of my burned café

but security pulled up beside me
screaming
"No stopping!"

slowly
lifting my foot off the brake

I drove
through
the open grave
of our town

No

Just because I live here
where it burned
just because
you see trauma on my face
just because I'm alone

it does not mean
you can message me
or buy gifts for my daughter
or call me
drunk
at midnight

Call your wife

One

The first time
I visited my Klowa
my ruins

two months
after the fire

I wasn't allowed past the sidewalk

"Too dangerous"
they said

half-fallen walls
unsteady bricks

the sifting organization
said sifting was unsafe

picked a few teacups from the edges

permitted me
to stand on the sidewalk
for a moment

gave me a bible

sent me away

100 days later

I agreed to an interview
on the six o'clock news

to raise my voice
for those who are here
surviving
on the edges

"Tell me about the fire"
he interrupted

reaching in
tearing out my nightmares
for public display

Line chart

A friend sent me a graphic
The Path of Collective Trauma

and I studied that little line
its sudden uphill surge
into community euphoria

(we'll rebuild we're resilient we're strong)

its change in direction

the plummet
                        down
            and down

the collective trauma
becomes
            individual suffering

down

like when you realize
they stole from the fundraiser
started in your name

or the Transportation Safety Board
says it wasn't their fault
that spark beside the tracks

when the cold winds arrive

and money runs out

        down

when the little support
you had to begin with
is gone

      down

when you see visible pain
on others' faces
at the gathering
at the protest

or when you can't do anything
except lie on the couch
and your child pats your shoulder

      down

when you ask for help
politely
      considerately
but receive none

and then you ask
tearfully
      begging
and they answer
"Well, if you could ask
in an adult way"

      down

until there is no money
no community
no support
no love
no hope

nothing

except this five-year-old girl
snuggled beside you
who depends upon you

and gives you a reason
the only reason
to live

Echo

In the absence of memory:
silence

just their voices

    "Don't go home, don't go home"
    and in their eyes I can see
    my house
    already
        burning

their voices
shimmering flames

and silence

a silent street, silent cars, silent faces
silent
    roaring
        fire

then
five months later
the loud cackle of a fire truck
sends me to the floor
        diving for cover
tangled breath
back-shaking tears

the surprise of sound
emerging from buried memory

from the silence

from the absence

Flood

The forest stabilizes the mountainside,
they say
so when the trees have burned
and the sky turns into a river

the blackened pines let go

water rushes down
earth rushes down
mountain rushes down

the highways wash out
on every side
and we're trapped

the school will be closed
until roads reopen
the roads will be closed
for months

the little stability we had
in this uncertain new life
has washed away

and I am reminded
                again
that we are unsafe
in this unstable world

Stranger

I didn't trust you at first

another one,
I thought
just sniffing for blood

I didn't tell you everything

I told you about strength, resilience
Community

but I didn't give you my tears

wet eyes watching yellow lines
with the remains of a town blurring through
the windows

Helen

At the sight of flames
in a cartoon haystack
she leapt over to me
covered my eyes
protected me

I asked her why

"Your face is scared when there's fire"

five years old
protecting me

The day of the fire
she wasn't home
she didn't see it
didn't run from it

but when I picked her up
I had changed
breaking
broken
her home
her normal
everything
changed

she clung tightly to me
afraid another separation
would mean another disaster

she clung tightly
for months

In the vulnerability of a messy bedroom
you asked her to cover my eyes
to protect me again

she reached up
                    her little hand
                                gentle over my eyes

I put an arm around her
held her
protected her
                    the best I could

Frozen

Barefoot on the winter lawn
with you
I laughed

said a symptom of shock was losing my shoes

Standing on the highway
heat rising off the asphalt
distorting the faces of unfamiliar men
officers

a dense grey-white pillar of smoke billowing above us
punctuated by black
explosions
homes

hearing
it will be months before we can go back

if there is anywhere left to go back to

looking down
at the surprise of bare feet
wondering if I had ever been wearing shoes
wondering if my feet were burning
feeling nothing

feeling

nothing

Ashes

Unfamiliar
 tenderness
when you leaned in
rolled my sleeve up slowly

my hands black and cold
covered in the ash
the burned forest
 a bag of it
that you brought
for my hands
to represent the trauma

you understood

a stranger

unknown
unexpected
intimate

the black dried on my hands
turned pale
 then white
ashen

ashes

you said
"Let's wash it off"
and leaned over me

warm water
dirt
 a black swirl down the drain

washing away the ash
washing away the trauma
with you
with goosebumps

Evening

There was this
        something

in the deepening dark

quiet voices
a hint of red wine

the absence of fire

this feeling
of
accepting each other
honestly
and always

In December

After you left
I looked at blank paper

         remembered years of silence
           suppression

picked up a pen

         and let them go

a letter to you

an act of expression
that broke apart the scar tissue
of the past

and led me to this

The letter

A grave man
          stiffly tall
his story wandering through past
and present
forgetting

nodded toward our snow-covered ruins
said
"Adversity is like travelling"

and I listened

                    comfort gone
                    normal
                          gone

Meeting you

reminded me of travelling
searching for somewhere
I belong

not here
buried under ten years of
roles
good daughter wife mother
stifling
uncomfortable
layers

searching for somewhere I belong
and instead
          finding
               someone

meeting you
reminded me of who I am

travelling does that

adversity
           does that

Finding you
      reminded me

to face this adversity
with integrity

to be vulnerable
      exposed
           honest

  and grateful

Snow

Snowflakes
fall in time to the simple chords
of the piano

peaceful arpeggios
spin softly

pine boughs slump
achingly
with the weight of the snow

in quiet mourning
for those trees that are gone
for those charred stumps
that remain

still

beneath the layer of white
all seems calm
subdued

snow falls in time
to the broken chords

covering
the poignancy of colour
the pain

Winter

There was no way to leave
with the highways washed out

the town roads impassable
because the snowplows
burned

and the snow too deep
to dig a path out of the driveway

so we stayed in the house

we ran out of firewood
in a house without heaters
awoke to a window
                    splintering
in jagged cold

we knew
   with the weight of the snow
the roof might collapse

but there was no way to leave

so we stayed in the house

and watched
another winter storm
move in

Morning

I want to reach out
to be surrounded by friends
by love

instead
with tears in my eyes
I am making pancakes
from a box
for a squalling child
in a burned-up town

broken
and alone
on Christmas day

Contents

A thick swamp
of insurance paperwork
on the kitchen floor

list after list

everything that was there
on the day it all burned

I can't work on the lists

can't think of each item
and remember

and imagine it there

in flames

At home

I long for a moment
uninterrupted

to finish the half-formed
thoughts
that hang in the air

to set down the burden of
parenting

    too heavy
               alone

to breathe deeply
and quietly

just once

Two

The second time
I visited my ruins
was in the spring

nine months after the fire

the dangerous walls
still standing

the loose bricks
more
                settled

the ash and debris
the same

a friend climbed into the basement
            pit of ashes
with a hand rake

sifted for hours

uncovering relics
of my past

broken sculpture
fractured china
rusted jewellery
embedded in pieces of shattered glass

I sat at the top
watched what she pulled out
feeling nothing
except a dull curiosity

how a burned doorknob looks like a vase
or knitting needles crumble with touch
or only the ugliest dishes survive

feeling dull curiosity
but no attachment
to this excavation
of life

she brought up jars
herb-infused salts
products I made in the kitchen
a few days before the fire

the glass still intact
just scorched

she set them gently
on the sidewalk
beside me

and one by one

I smashed them

On location

They filmed a commercial
in the ruins of our town

two small girls
              walking on sunshine

happy little journey
past our chimneys and ashes
our gaping basements
our hollow shells

two little girls
and a large film crew
stopping traffic
in our burned-up town

where we are not allowed
to open car windows
or walk our own streets

but are made to idle and wait
and watch
while they film

Rules

Keep your windows up,
they say

don't breathe in the cloud of dust
don't breathe in the toxins

(oh no, there's no dust now, but one day there could be)

Keep your windows up,
they say

don't look past the yellow line
don't look through that security fence
don't look at those crumbled buildings
don't look at the piles of ash

don't look at us while we clean this up
don't look at us while we stand
                              and laugh

Keep your windows up,
they say

don't look at us

don't breathe

Trains

Oh yes,
we can hear the metal
shrieking

all the way through the canyon

don't think we don't know
about those sparks

Return

When I opened the door
you smiled
stepped inside

and despite the fatigue
of travel
and the awkwardness of distance

you looked at me
honestly

saw me
beneath the layers

and asked how I've been

Three

The third time
was with you

eleven months after the fire

ash and rubble
condensed by snow
washed by rain
but still, debris

you brought your cameras
documenting

and I

I made my way
over scattered bricks
sat down on pieces of a fallen wall
where once there were tables
people
in summer sunshine

that third time
I let the memories pass through me
moments
echoes
of that burned place

I saw my daughter's first steps
heard the laughter in the kitchen
felt the agony of divorce
there

staring at a rusted steel door
I remembered how that heat sealer
never quite fit anywhere
      heavy pain in the ass
now solidly holding up a crumpled door
for eleven months

there, with you,
I opened myself to the memories
because I was open to you

the sunlight greyed

rain fell

when you sat on the cold bricks beside me
I picked a piece of ivy
survivor
remnant of the vines
that I planted and watched grow
for years

you tucked it in your pocket
buttoned it in
safe, protected
survivor

and when there was nothing
left to remember
we stood up
walked across debris
drove away

Today
the ivy grows in water
on my windowsill

slowly

Fragment

A poem that will hurt
to be written

I fled the fire
went straight to their house
the house I was born into
the house

no not yet

Sage

The smell of my childhood:
warm sagebrush
beside the river

with the feeling of
bare feet
on soft sand

When you told me
you didn't know the smell of sage
I took you to the hillside
showed you the fragrant grey kAwquoo[1]

                          (far-from-water)
and you breathed in deeply

I remembered
when the whole town was burning
and we were running
for our lives

how the wind was carrying flames
upriver
       both rivers

the fire was roaring
along riverbanks
up hillsides
into mountains
through homes

and the air was filled with the smell
of burning sage

---

1 *kAwquoo* is the name for big sagebrush (*Artemisia tridentada*) in the
Nlaka'pamux language

Up Nicomen

In the mountains
you picked morels for us

bountiful burn scar

gift of the fire

Highway 12

One night
in the darkness
child asleep
you beside me

the familiar winding road
following the river

going home

I drove slowly
to watch for deer on the edges
and to prolong the quiet sweetness
of being with you

lost in your voice

lost
in the feeling

we rounded a corner
where I half expected to see
the sparkling lights of a town

and saw the black anguish of
darkness

nothing

an absence
        bigger than the night
that pulled me out of the moment
                        out of the intimacy
and into the trauma

I reached for your hand
                (please pull me back in)

I reached for your hand
for the first time

TLK̲emchEEn

"I was wondering
if you'd like to have coffee
at the beach
in the morning"

and I was shaking
with nerves
at the thought

and you said yes

There
at the place
where two rivers
meet
high water reaching up into the bushes
from either side
and pushing out
                    down
with the current

we found a patch of sand
laid a blanket
sat together

the sound of two rivers
joining
with our voices

the burned town just above us
out of sight

In that sacred place

where we learn to look upstream
   giving thanks
for what will be given

to watch the current flow past
   letting go
of what we can't control

I let the water take my fear
and told you
my feelings

and you shared yours

and the two rivers
flowed together
into one

The body

A poem about the body
our bodies

about your skin against mine

because the body holds the trauma
until it lets go
in something beyond vulnerability
beyond honesty

deep

    truth

the weight of your body against me

and the weight you give mine:
you ground me,
connect me

you show me my depth

outside there might be fire
there might be ash

but inside

here in this
softness

there is the joy
of
discovery
of pleasure

of forgetting, and remembering

of you
and me

together

In June

We held warm cups of coffee
in the dim morning light

your cameras packed away
with photos of us

a quiet moment
a goodbye

and you went back to New York

no sorrow

there is no sorrow
in the knowledge of love

the only time I cried
    with you

was when you called me beautiful

Anniversary

There are so many
memories
and stories
today

I try to react to them all
without reading any
of the words

because we have been thinking
about this day
every day
for a year

I scroll through
the stories
and
      absently
pause to watch a video
with the volume up

and stop breathing

flooded
by the memory of sound

and flame

and smoke

and fear

Distance

We step straight in
to a world that is
intimate
and infinite

instead of stumbling around
in awkward small places

your words give me space
to think about art
writing

healing

in the sound of your voice
I am protected
beloved

Fabric

Yesterday
I knit again
wrapped yarn over needles

   black cotton
   dyed with iron
       rusty nails

I haven't knit
not since the fire
not since it all burned
in futility

but yesterday
I saw the smoke rising off the hillside
and knit it
row by row
layering colour upon colour
picking up
painting
with thread

the image
burning my mind
being translated through my hands

dropped stitches
disrupted fabric
intentional deconstruction
    damage

when it was finished
off the needles
I tried it on, this piece of smoke
and choked
panicked
ripped it off my neck

sudden revulsion
sudden reaction
to the slow process
of recreating
     my nightmare
stitch by stitch

Normal

We walk to school
holding hands

under layers of mountains
    wind
        and sky

she tells stories
sings songs

and together we search
for the smoothest
white stones

I can't hear
the machinery
scraping our town away

    if I don't listen

I can't see the shadows

if I don't look

Nohomin fire

Do you remember
when you were in France
and there were fireworks
on the midnight beach

and I was here
in hot midday sun

and as we talked
I saw smoke
across the river

a puff
a soft cloud
and then a black billow
a raging monster
devouring farms and homes
before I could blink

and I told you
"There's another fire"
and tried to close the blinds
so I wouldn't see it
but my hands were shaking

while in Antibes
a cooling breeze
blew softly
from
the

sea

Without you

Feeling the loss of you
even though you're not gone
you're where you always were

far away
        too far

in those brief moments
that you were here
the ache was softness
the absence was possibility
I was
        me

and now you're gone

the loss of you is so wide
it feels like I've lost myself
again

I want you
I want you to be here
close to me

and you're too far away

too far to reach across,
you say
too far to even try,
you say
too far

the loss of you is too deep

I don't want to lose you
I don't want to lose
        me

Mud

I was buried
in sadness
by your words

unable to breathe
to lift the weight off my lungs

choking
on the heavy clay of agony
suffocating
with tears

as I cried
the pain
pushed me deeper into the earth

it was you
and it was more than you

I was stuck
in the memories of fire
the despair
struggling life

suffering
deeply

the thick black dirt
of sorrow
mixing with tears
to become
liberating
grief

A dedication

This poetry is for you
but not for the person you are today
the one who just broke my heart
the one who stepped forward
then back
the one who

I was writing it for you
for the person who saw me
recognized me
valued me

and then you didn't

you shouldn't have kissed me
crossed over to where feelings
weighed more than complications
you shouldn't have
if you were always going to step back

This poetry isn't for you.

I was writing it for you
but it was always just for me

Purification

I hold a match
to a piece of sage
spark of flame
smoulders
goes out

the fragrant
          blur
of cleansing smoke
  drifts up

I hold a match
watch the flame
grow

orange
blue
flickering

fire

burning

filling the air
with black
murderous
smoke

growing

the room is on fire
the house is on fire
the town is on fire

burning

until nothing is left

no present
no future
no breath
no
    life

just ashes
that blow away
in hot summer wind

nothing is left

except

    truth

Sharing

I wrote a post
about the past year
the lonely impossibility
of it all

mentioned
that due to bureaucratic delays
my insurance isn't enough to rebuild

said
maybe healing
and maybe art

but Klowa's doors are closed

and the world reached out

to thank me for that space
to hold me in my mourning
to lift me with support

the strength of community
through loss
and through grief
is the blanket
draped gently
over my shoulders

Sockeye

People are fishing today
the Nlaka'pamux
dipping their nets into strong water
hanging deep red flesh
to dry in the wind
almost like
life goes on

my neighbour brought me a salmon
heavy gift
almost like she had always been next door
almost like her house
didn't burn

I washed the dishes
sat down outside
watched a dry leaf shake
in the wind

almost like
I was ok

Now

AN EPILOGUE

Even when I was crushed
broken

crumpled on the floor

    I knew I was wrong

I knew the present
was too insubstantial
to be trusted at all

and you were never the way out
of this darkness
this burned-up place

I am

and now that I am breathing
    now that I am whole

I understand the bravery
of trusting
        connection

and I understand the strength
of trusting
myself

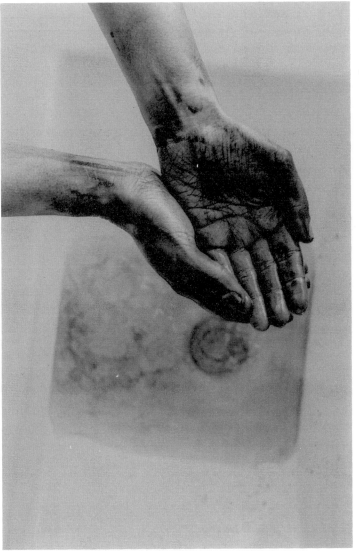

Acknowledgements

One morning, a year or so after the fire, I sat on the living room floor with the intention of recording a memory. The memory emerged as a poem, and tears, and the beginning of grieving, and it surprised me. But what surprised me more—and soon became more important than the act of writing itself—was the overwhelming need to share this poetry, to hear others' reactions to it, and to witness them reading their own experiences and emotions into my words.

So, thank you. Thank you for reading it now. Thank you to Caitlin Press for making this possible. And thank you to all those friends (too many to name, but each of you so appreciated) who read this book as it was being written; no one could come over for tea without being handed a stack of poems. Your feedback encouraged me to keep writing, to keep sharing.

I am grateful to Larissa Thomson, Bev Phillips and Emma-Lee Joe, for your editing, language guidance and cultural sensitivity reading, respectively. To Alejandro Alvarez, Shannon Story and Aaron Wulf, the first three strangers to read the book; you showed me that the story could reach beyond the edges of Lytton. To Martha Dippo and Robert King, who sat with coffee mugs and pages spread over the kitchen table, and to Jill McDermid, who talked it through on the phone until our voices were hoarse; your generous, thorough analyses helped me believe in the value of my writing. And to Rebecca Schwartz, the poetry superhero; you swooped in and vanquished the last of the crushing imposter syndrome.

I am also grateful to Murdock McIntyre, who ran into Klowa to tell us about the fire. To the Lytton Fire Department, BC Wildfire Service and the other firefighters who came to help: thank you for battling the monster and saving so much of our community. To Deanna Porter and NaomiBelle Rozell, for keeping Helen safe in the first days after the fire. To everyone who sent messages of concern and support; even when I wasn't able to write you back, I read every word and felt your love. And to all of you across the province and around the world who sent donations and letters and kindness to Lytton, thank you.

Thank you to Bev Hutchinson, for sharing my excitement, being a hopeless romantic, and helping me change some core beliefs.

You're right, even if it took me a while to see it: *intense* really can mean "beautiful."

Thank you to Micha Kingston, for the play dates and long conversations and knowing what it means to be a single parent after disaster. I admire the strength and compassion that you have cultivated even after you lost so much to the fire, and I can't wait for you and Mimi to come home again.

Thank you to Benjamin Salesse, for arriving when you did and listening so closely. For seeing the beauty in this grief-stricken place and capturing it in your photos. For nodding when I told you "I'm a writer," even though I hadn't written a word in ten years. Thank you for inspiring so much.

Thank you to Kendra Grahauer, for being there through every moment. For folding Helen into your flock and keeping us nourished and loved during the month-long shock of evacuation. For answering every phone call from me before and since, and hearing the words behind my tears. For knowing me forever and understanding me completely, and for helping me realize that my writing voice is me.

Thank you to the people of Lytton—from the Nlaka'pamux (nlha.kApmhh) communities of Nicomen, Skuppah, Siska, Kanaka and Lytton First Nation; from the Village proper; and from Gladwin, Botanie, West Side and beyond—those who lost their homes to the fire and those who are still here. Each one of you is an example of what it means to keep going, together.

And, most of all, thank you to Helen. You are teaching me things I never knew about love. I feel so lucky to be your mom.

About the Author

Meghan Fandrich lives with her young daughter on the edge of Lytton, BC, the village that was destroyed by wildfire in 2021. She spent her childhood and much of her adult life there in Nlaka'pamux Territory, where two rivers meet and sagebrush-covered hills reach up into mountains. Before the fire she ran Klowa Art Café, a beloved and vibrant part of the community; Klowa was lost to the flames. *Burning Sage* is Meghan's debut poetry collection.

PHOTO BY SHELANNE JUSTICE